GI Joe in World War II

by Sharon Cromwell

Content Adviser: G. Kurt Piehler, Ph.D.,
Associate Professor of History,
University of Tennessee, Knoxville

Reading Adviser: Rosemary G. Palmer, Ph.D.,
Department of Literacy, College of Education,
Boise State University

Compass Point Books ✦ Minneapolis, Minnesota

Compass Point Books
151 Good Counsel Drive
P.O. Box 669
Mankato, MN 56002-0669

 This book was manufactured with paper containing at least 10 percent post-consumer waste.

On the cover: U.S. soldier in Normandy after D-Day during World War II

Photographs ©: Bob Landry/Time & Life Pictures/Getty Images, cover; Prints Old & Rare, back cover (far left); Library of Congress, back cover, 28, 33, 34; Courtesy of Army Art Collection, U.S. Army Center of Military History, 5; U.S. Coast Guard/Time & Life Pictures/Getty Images, 6; Fred Ramage/ Keystone/Getty Images, 7; AP Images, 9, 16; Myron Davis/Time & Life Pictures/Getty Images, 12; Dmitri Kessel/Time & Life Pictures/Getty Images, 13; R. Gates/Hulton Archive/Getty Images, 14; Hulton Archive/Getty Images, 18, 29; The Granger Collection, New York, 19; David E. Scherman/Time & Life Pictures/Getty Images, 20; MPI/Getty Images, 22; U.S. Army/Getty Images, 23; STF/AFP/Getty Images, 25; Lambert/Getty Images, 30; Margaret Bourke-White/Time & Life Pictures/Getty Images, 31; Lenny Ignelzi/AP Images, 36; Morry Gash/AP Images, 37; U.S. Signal Corps/Time & Life Pictures/Getty Images, 38; Photos 12/Alamy, 39; Gary C. Knapp/AP Images, 40; Patrick Baz/AFP/ Getty Images, 41.

Editor: Anthony Wacholtz
Art Director/Page Production: LuAnn Ascheman-Adams
Photo Researcher: Robert McConnell
Cartographer: XNR Productions, Inc.
Library Consultant: Kathleen Baxter

Creative Director: Keith Griffin
Editorial Director: Nick Healy
Managing Editor: Catherine Neitge

Library of Congress Cataloging-in-Publication Data
Cromwell, Sharon, 1947–
  GI Joe in World War II / by Sharon Cromwell.
    p. cm.—(We the people)
  Includes index.
  ISBN 978-0-7565-3842-2 (library binding)
  1. World War, 1939–1945—United States—Juvenile literature. 2. Soldiers—United States—History—20th century—Juvenile literature. I. Title. II. Series.
  D769.C76 2008
  940.54'1273—dc22   2008005729

Visit Compass Point Books on the Internet at *www.compasspointbooks.com* or e-mail your request to *custserv@compasspointbooks.com*

TABLE OF CONTENTS

STORMING THE BEACHES

On the morning of June 6, 1944—a date known as D-Day—a vast armada of ships carried U.S., British, Canadian, and French troops from England to the beaches of Normandy in northern France. This largest sea invasion in history would eventually lead to the defeat of the Germans and the end of World War II.

Overhead, Allied aircraft bombed and weakened the German positions before the invading troops reached the beaches. The large guns on the U.S. warships also tried to blow up German defenses on the coast. Chilly, frightened, and seasick, U.S. soldiers—also known as GIs—crowded together in their small landing boats that cut through the churning sea.

Carrying 75-pound (33.8-kilogram) battle packs, GIs struggled through the surf and stormed Omaha Beach, one of the five Allied landing sites. Artillery and machine-gun fire rained down on them from German troops. From an

GIs huddled behind the protective metal front of the landing craft as they neared shore.

elevated position, German soldiers dug themselves into
trenches, making it hard for the GIs to get clear shots.
As the troops advanced farther up the beach, hidden land
mines exploded, killing and injuring many soldiers.

Despite the unfavorable situation, the GIs pushed on,
while the German troops fought hard to keep the invading
soldiers from getting a toehold onshore. By nightfall,

After leaving the landing crafts, the GIs waded through the water and fought their way onto the beaches of Normandy.

however, the Allied troops had taken the beaches. Although the Germans had prepared the beaches for an invasion, the D-Day landing had surprised them. The seas had been rough on June 5, and the Germans did not expect an attack from the water.

More than 9,000 Allied soldiers were dead or wounded, but more than 100,000 troops were ashore. Fighting the

Germans for every bit of ground, the troops began to move inland. The German army proved tough to beat, and the war would continue for another year. But the Allies' strategic invasion and the bravery of the American GIs would move the Allies one step closer to winning the war.

The GIs encountered German tanks after moving inland from the beaches.

7

WORLD WAR II AND THE GIS

During World War II, 16 million men and 500,000 women served in the U.S. Army, Navy, Army Air Force, Coast Guard, or Marines. About 60 percent of the men were drafted, or required to serve. The rest—including all of the women—were volunteers.

The foot soldiers in the Army were dubbed "GI Joes." The name GI Joe came from a cartoon in the Army magazine *Yank*. Artist and soldier David Breger used his own experiences to create the GI Joe comic. He showed what was funny about the soldier's life.

Breger took the initials "GI" from the Army. GI, which stood for "Government Issue," was stamped on Army supplies such as canteens, shoes, and soldiers' uniforms. GI also described the soldiers' short haircut and almost anything else related to the Army. The U.S. soldiers who became known as GIs played a huge part in winning the war.

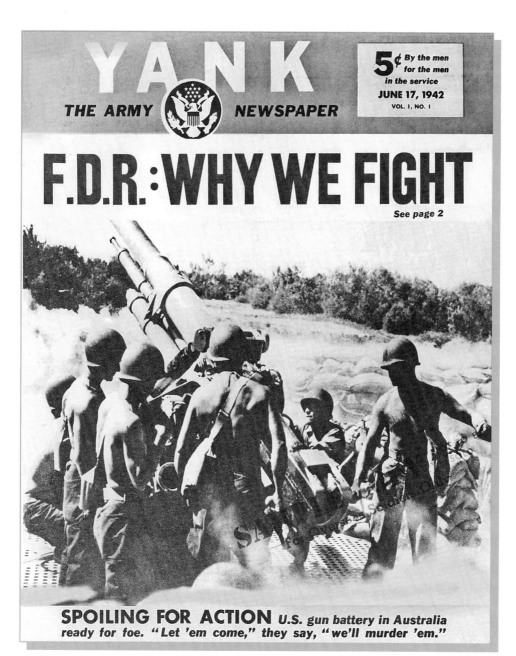

The first issue of Yank *featured American soldiers in Australia and included greetings from President Franklin D. Roosevelt.*

About the War

World War II was a global conflict that lasted from 1939 to 1945. Battles were fought in Europe, northern Africa, the Middle East, southwest Asia, China, and the Pacific Ocean.

The United States, Great Britain, France, the Soviet Union, and other countries were known as the Allies. The Allies fought against the main Axis powers—Germany, Italy, and Japan.

The war began when Adolf Hitler, the dictator of Nazi Germany, invaded Poland in 1939. He saw Germans as a "master race" that was fit to rule the world. For this reason, he wanted to exterminate all Jews, which led to the Holocaust—the genocide of European Jews and other minorities.

The United States entered the war in 1941 after the Japanese attacked its naval base in Pearl Harbor, Hawaii. The war ended in 1945 with the defeat of Germany and Japan. More than 50 million people died worldwide, making it the deadliest war in history.

10

After the United States entered World War II following the Pearl Harbor bombing, many men volunteered to join the Army, Navy, Army Air Force, Marines, or Coast Guard. Millions more men were drafted. Camps were set up for training them in warfare.

Before men left for training camp, they had to put their lives in order. That was usually easy for single men. For men with families, it was more difficult. Family men tried to make sure there was money in the bank for their wives to use on household expenses. They asked other family members and friends to help their families when necessary.

Many men took troop trains to reach their training camps. Most of these trains carried thousands of men. The men traded life stories and got to know one another while traveling. After they got off the trains and settled into their training camps, they soon realized they faced huge changes.

GIs in training camps woke up before sunrise. They learned to shoot rifles and practiced climbing, running, and crawling on the ground—all skills they would need in battle.

Before a day of intense training, recruits warmed up with exercises, such as jumping jacks, that loosened and strengthened their muscles.

Through the intense weeks of training, the GIs continued to learn more about one another.

In training camps, many GIs ate more food than they ever had before. They had hot chocolate, canned meat, orange juice, tinned and fresh fruit, soft drinks, candy, and chewing gum.

The average GI was in his mid-20s and was born around the time World War I ended in 1918. He was roughly 5 feet 8 inches (172 centimeters) tall and

Recruits worked on their aim at a firing range as part of their basic training.

weighed 150 pounds (67.5 kilograms). He had finished one year of high school—three to four years more than the average soldier in World War I.

Although most GIs were men, women volunteered their skills to help win the war. Hundreds of thousands of women joined the Women's Army Corps (WAC) and the Navy's Women Accepted for Voluntary Emergency Service

*Women volunteers loaded into the back of a military truck
and prepared to leave for North Africa.*

(WAVES). WACs performed more than 200 jobs in the war,
including serving as secretaries and telephone operators.

Women also joined a Coast Guard reserves program
called SPARS—a contraction of the Coast Guard motto
"Semper Paratus" and its English translation, "Always
Ready." The Women Air Force Service Pilots (WASP), a
civilian organization designed to help the Army Air Force

ferry planes around the country, also helped train male pilots.

Both male and female GIs came from many backgrounds. Soldiers who had grown up in Italian, Irish, Polish, or Hispanic neighborhoods learned to work and train together. Men with various religious backgrounds set aside their differences to fight for a common cause.

However, not all of the troops were allowed to train together. During most of the war, African-Americans in the armed forces were segregated. African-Americans had fought bravely in previous wars, but at the start of World War II, the Army would not send black soldiers into battle. And at first, the Army Air Force and the Marine Corps would not let blacks enlist.

Although the tension from being segregated lasted throughout the war, the soldiers' differences had to be put aside to focus on the fighting. The GIs soon had a chance to put their intense training to use. They would face the German and Italian armies in North Africa.

15

GI JOE IN NORTH AFRICA

Under the command of General Dwight D. Eisenhower, enormous ships carried GIs from the United States to North Africa in 1942. Each soldier carried a rifle, a bedroll, a canteen, canned rations (food called c-rations), a few

U.S. General Dwight Eisenhower (left) and General Henri Giraud, commander of the French forces, rode together to a base in Tunis in North Africa.

personal items, and anything else he needed. For combat, they donned a 1-pound (.45-kilogram) steel helmet that also could be used for several other purposes, such as a basin or cooking pot. Their uniforms were made of wool and cotton, and they contained several pockets to hold items the GI would need. The soldiers wore heavy boots that helped them walk over rough terrain.

At night in North Africa, GIs slept in foxholes they dug in the ground, putting tents over them to protect themselves from rain and wind. GIs decorated their living quarters with photos of their girlfriends and family members to remind them of home.

GIs marched miles and miles through valleys and over hills to reach battles. Equipped with as many weapons and as much ammunition as they could carry, many of the soldiers claimed they were so tired that they slept as they walked. At times, they fought for days on end and did not even have time to eat their c-rations, which were canned foods such as vegetable-and-meat hash. Their pace was

The hilly terrain in North Africa made traveling difficult for the GIs.

often too fast to allow the kitchen crew to set up their equipment and provide a hot meal.

In the field, if GIs had coffee or hot chocolate, they had to drink it just before bedtime. They had to make fires in their foxholes, where they would not be spotted by the enemy. They brewed coffee or heated hot chocolate on small stoves they had in their foxholes.

GIs did not have enough water to take baths or wash

A GI attempted to bail out his foxhole after a rainstorm.

their uniforms for weeks or months. They didn't shave much because of the small amount of water they had each day. Still, they found interesting ways to use shaving cream. They put it on their skin to soothe sunburn and windburn or to kill fleas that bit them.

The conditions were not much better for the women in North Africa. Many of them worked as nurses, caring for wounded GIs in large hospital tents. Some were close to the

19

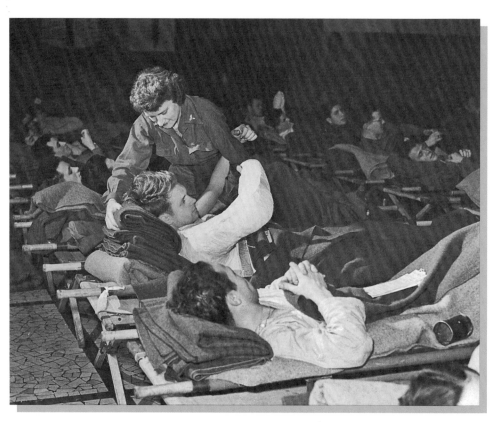

Nurses worked many hours attending to the wounded GIs. Cots in the hospital tents were positioned in long rows to accommodate the growing number of injured soldiers.

fighting, and enemy artillery often ripped through the tents, while bombs exploded nearby. Doctors and nurses risked their lives to care for the GIs.

Max B. Siegel, a rifleman and an ammunition carrier for machine guns in North Africa, later recalled the depressing situation there. The morning after a tough battle, he wrote in his diary that there was "too much chow [and] nobody to eat it" because so many soldiers had died.

To keep their spirits up, GIs did not talk about war all the time. Instead, they talked about home. Many of the GIs believed they would return home by April 1943, so they continued to fight with the hope of soon ending the war.

The Allies fought the Axis forces in North Africa into May 1943. A combined American and British force of 65,000 troops pushed the Axis armies from western to eastern North Africa. The U.S. Army Air Force had bombed German and Italian troops to weaken their armies before the GIs arrived. On May 13, 1943, the Axis forces surrendered to the Allies in Tunisia. The Allies captured 250,000 Germans and Italians.

GI JOE IN ITALY

After the victory in North Africa, U.S. President Franklin D. Roosevelt and British leader Winston Churchill decided Italy should be the next target. The Allies attacked the island of Sicily in July 1943. Allied troops invaded the mainland of Italy from the south and drove Axis troops north.

While some of the GIs were knee-deep in mud in the valleys, other GIs climbed steep mountains in bad winter weather to fight the Italians and Germans. GIs often tried to rest at night in the mountains, where snow was

Several GIs strained to push their jeep through muddy terrain in Italy.

22

falling and the temperature was below freezing. Ernie Pyle, a well-known reporter who traveled with the GIs, wrote, "They had no blankets to keep them warm, no beds but the rocks. And they did it without complaining. The human spirit is an astounding thing."

Horses and mules carried food and ammunition to GIs on mountaintops after trucks could go no higher. When

Four American soldiers strapped their machine guns and ammunition to a pack mule before traveling through the mountains.

the horses and mules could not go farther, men took up supplies on their backs.

At times, mail was brought with the supplies. Reading mail from home was the best part of any GI's day. A handwritten letter from a loved one kept up the soldiers' morale. Some letters had to be carried back down the mountains and returned to their senders because they were sent to men who had been killed in battle.

Over time, U.S. Army Air Force planes ruled the sky during the fighting. As in North Africa, bombing weakened the German troops and helped the GIs move ahead. Still, it was slow going for the Allied troops. The Germans blew up bridges as they retreated, and GIs had to rebuild them to keep moving north. The German and Italian troops fought hard to stop the GIs from taking Italy, but Italy surrendered in September 1943. In all, 188,000 Americans and 123,000 British troops were killed or injured in Italy.

GI JOE IN FRANCE

The invasion of France on D-Day in 1944 began the Allied push across Europe toward Germany. As GIs forced the Germans back into the French countryside, the Germans left snipers behind to slow the Allied progress. Snipers hid

GIs tried to locate the gunfire from a German sniper in Saint-Malo, France.

25

in the hedgerows—lines of tall, bushy shrubs that separated fields—and shot to kill. Snipers were hard to find and killed many soldiers. The only way to deal with snipers was to pursue and kill them one by one.

GIs in constant battle got little sleep. Ernie Pyle wrote about one group of soldiers he was with in France that had less than four hours of rest in three solid days of intense battles.

Fighting hard all the way, U.S. soldiers pushed German troops out of most of northwestern France. GIs later fought the Germans in Belgium and Luxembourg. In the Battle of the Bulge, U.S. troops stopped the Germans from moving back into France.

Paris was liberated from German armed forces on August 25, 1944. The people of Paris took to the streets to celebrate. They hugged, kissed, and cheered GIs who rode down city streets.

The Allies then pushed into Germany at its western border. Soviet troops captured Berlin, the German capital, and Nazi leader Adolf Hitler killed himself in despair.

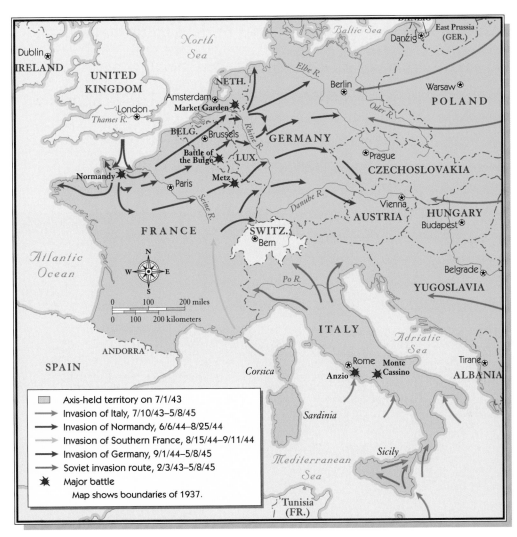

The Allied push into Europe during World War II required several separate invasions.

Germany surrendered in May 1945, and the war's focus then turned to defeating Japan. The Japanese had wiped out many U.S. Navy ships when they bombed Pearl Harbor.

Japan had also taken over most of the islands west of Hawaii in the Pacific Ocean.

The Allies had been pushing the Japanese back toward Japan since the spring of 1942. In June 1942, U.S. forces won the important Battle of Midway Island.

U.S. Navy fighter planes attacked the Japanese fleet during the Battle of Midway.

At Midway, the Japanese had hoped to destroy the entire U.S. Pacific Fleet.

In August 1945, the United States dropped two atomic bombs on Japan, and the Soviet Union entered the war against the Japanese. Japan surrendered on September 2, marking the end of World War II. Putting aside

The single-word headline of a Stars and Stripes *newspaper proclaimed that World War II was over.*

the death and destruction they had witnessed during the war, American GIs were thrilled to finally head home to their families and friends.

RETURNING HOME

GIs returned to a country that was doing well. U.S. factories that built products for the war also made a variety of products for regular citizens after the war. New cars, refrigerators, washing machines, clothes, furniture, and many other items were for sale, and many people bought them. Most returning soldiers found jobs. They had money to buy even more products that factory workers made.

A grateful nation wanted to help return-ing GIs get good jobs

A soldier returning from the war was excitedly embraced at a train station.

and homes. The GI Bill of Rights, which had become law in 1944, paid for GIs to finish high school, attend college, enroll in medical school, study at foreign universities, or learn new jobs. Veterans also had the opportunity to obtain low-cost loans to purchase homes.

War veterans took notes during a class lecture at the University of Iowa in 1947.

31

Many GIs had never dreamed of graduating from college or getting job training. They found higher-paying work than they had before the war. Low-interest loans helped GIs buy homes and start businesses. By the time the program ended in July 1956, millions of GIs had taken part in education or training. A newer version of the GI Bill continues to provide benefits to former soldiers.

During the war, women held jobs in factories and shipyards to replace the men serving in the armed forces. But after the war, most women had to give back those jobs to returning GIs. Many mothers went back to home-making and full-time care for their children. Some women continued to work as teachers or in offices and stores. Other women disliked giving up their wartime jobs. In factories and shipyards, they had earned better pay than they had from jobs that were mostly done by women.

As time passed, more women worked as lawyers, doctors, and businesspeople. Women often combined these other careers with marriage and motherhood. Eventually

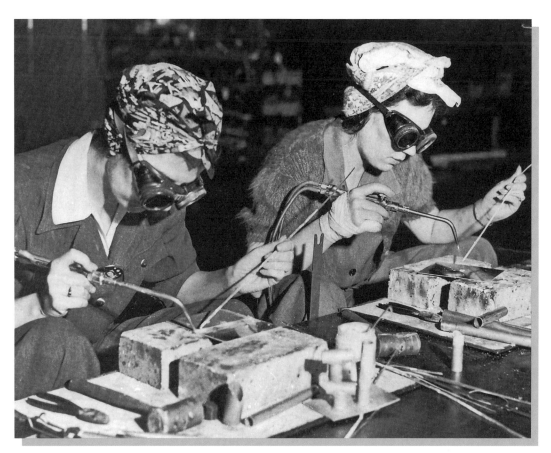

Many of the women who had worked on assembly lines during the war were forced to give up their jobs for the men returning from overseas.

women were able to work at the same jobs as men. The role women took in World War II—at home and overseas—was a crucial push for women's rights.

The rights of African-Americans were also addressed during World War II. Although they would

33

continue to face racial discrimination for many years to come, African-Americans made a move toward equality during the war. By the end of 1944, the Army had 4,500 black soldiers fighting alongside white soldiers. The Navy included about 500 black seamen on ships. The Army Air Force added black pilots—the Tuskegee Airmen—who

African-American aviators at the Tuskegee Army Air Field in Alabama

became heroes. Starting in 1942, the Marine Corps trained an all-African-American fighting force. In 1948, President Harry S. Truman ordered desegregation of the armed forces. Other American institutions would eventually follow suit.

GIs learned about other countries and acquired new skills during the war, but most of all, they learned a lot about their fellow Americans. When they returned to the United States, they brought with them a greater understanding of people of other ethnic and religious backgrounds. Some GIs settled back into their old neighborhoods, happy with what they knew. Others moved to new regions of the country, looking for change in their future. All of the GIs, however, were affected by the important role they played in the war.

GI Joe in U.S. Culture

Although GI Joe was the name given to U.S. soldiers in World War II, it also became a national icon. In 1964, the U.S. toy company Hasbro began producing military action figures. At first, there was an action soldier, an action sailor, an action pilot, and an action Marine. GI Joe was no longer just a nickname for the average U.S. soldier—it was a line of action figures.

As years passed, the GI Joe action figures began to change. They have ranged in size from 12 inches (30.5 centimeters) to 2½ inches (6.4 cm) tall. The action figures' missions also changed over time.

The original GI Joe action figure was created by Don Levine for Hasbro Toys.

36

Around 1970, during the height of the unpopular Vietnam War, Hasbro wanted to downplay the war theme. Instead of a World War II soldier, GI Joe became the leader of an adventure team that fought evil.

In 1982, Hasbro created a GI Joe line called A Real American Hero—a name that would eventually define the line of toys. The first issue of *GI Joe: A Real American Hero!* comic books appeared that same year. The comic books, which were published by Marvel Comics, were based on the new line of GI Joe action figures.

A code name and specialty were assigned to each Real American Hero action figure.

In the following decades, the action figures' missions became more specialized. In 1991, Hasbro created the GI Joe Eco-Warriors line to call attention to the environment. The next year, the Drug Elimination Force line of figures was produced.

The real and fictional experiences of GI Joe have been used in other kinds of entertainment as well. In 1945, a hit movie, *The Story of G.I. Joe*, played in theaters. It was based on the experiences of war reporter Ernie Pyle as he followed U.S. troops in North Africa and Italy, where he was killed by a sniper's bullet.

Ernie Pyle (1900–1945)

In 1985 and 1986, *GI Joe: A Real American Hero*—an animated GI

Joe series—was shown on television. It was based on the toy line and the comic books. Another animated series with the same name appeared on TV from 1989 to 1991.

Movies have also been made using the popular World War II nickname. *GI Joe: The Movie* is a 1987 animated film that was released as a video. The title of the 1997 movie *GI Jane*, which starred Demi Moore, is a play on the name GI Joe. The movie is based on a fictional female character who trains to become the first woman in a specialized division of the Navy.

In GI Jane, Demi Moore's character endured intense physical and mental training to become the first female Navy SEAL.

GI Joe figures have been popular toys for more than 40 years. There are more than 250 GI Joe comic books, and there are several GI Joe video games as well. In 2004, GI Joe entered the National Toy Hall of Fame. Three years later, in 2007, Hasbro marked the 25th anniversary of the Real American Hero line of GI Joe figures. To commemorate the event, the toy company released an anniversary

A collector proudly displayed an assortment of more than 160 GI Joe action figures and hundreds of outfits, vehicles, and other accessories.

In 2004, a U.S. Marine carried a GI Joe doll with him while serving in Iraq.

collection of 3¾-inch (9.5-cm) figures. Today some GI Joe action figures and comic books are collector's items.

However, the fantasy world of GI Joe is vastly different from the real world of the GIs in World War II. The GIs had a tough job. They slept out in the cold and walked for many miles without rest. Many died or were wounded in battle. What those GIs did for the United States and the world will never be forgotten.

GLOSSARY

armada—large group of moving things, such as ships

collector's items—things that a collector saves that can be valuable

c-rations—enough food in one can to last a GI one day

discrimination—unfair treatment of a person or group, often because of race or religion

drafted—compelled by law to serve in the military

ethnic—relating to a group of people sharing the same national origins, language, history, or culture

line—group of things that share common traits, such as a line of toys

recruits—new members of the armed forces

segregate—to separate groups of people based on their race

DID YOU KNOW?

- U.S. factory workers helped win World War II. By the end of the war, U.S. factories had made about 5,750 merchant ships, 1,500 naval vessels, 300,000 aircraft, 635,000 jeeps, 88,500 tanks, 11,000 chain saws, 2.3 million trucks, 6.5 million rifles, and 40 billion bullets.

- GIs often put names on their equipment. A GI might carve his name or initials—or the name of his wife or girlfriend—on his rifle.

- Army schools taught almost a million recruits in the armed forces how to read and write.

- Doctors fitted 2.25 million recruits with eyeglasses.

- Tents were set up overseas to provide services such as dentistry for the GIs.

43

IMPORTANT DATES

Timeline

1939	Nazi Germany invades Poland; World War II begins.
1940	The U.S. Selective Service and Training Act of 1940 applied to more than 16 million men between the ages of 21 and 36; some of them were drafted.
1941	Japan bombs the U.S. naval base at Pearl Harbor; the United States, Great Britain, and Canada declare war on Japan; Germany declares war on the United States.
1942	In June, Allied troops defeat Japan in the Battle of Midway in the Pacific; in November, GIs land in North Africa.
1943	In July, GIs land in Sicily; in September, Italy surrenders to the Allies.
1944	On D-Day, GIs and other Allied forces invade the north coast of France at Normandy; in August, GIs and Free French Forces liberate Paris; in October, the Allies defeat Japan's navy in the Philippines.
1945	In May, Germany surrenders; in August, Japan surrenders, and the GIs return home.

IMPORTANT PEOPLE

DAVID BREGER (1908–1970)

Soldier and creator of the GI Joe cartoon about the comic adventures of a foot soldier in World War II; Breger was promoted through the ranks to corporal, sergeant, and lieutenant; after the war, his cartoon "Mister Breger" ran daily in newspapers until 1969

DWIGHT D. EISENHOWER (1890–1969)

Commanding Army general during World War II; he led Allied forces in North Africa in 1942 and in France on D-Day in 1944; he was elected president in 1952

FRANKLIN D. ROOSEVELT (1882–1945)

President of the United States from 1933 to 1945, serving longer than any other president; he led the United States during its worst economic depression and most of World War II; he backed the building of the atomic bomb and the creation of the United Nations

HARRY S. TRUMAN (1884–1972)

President of the United States from 1945 to 1953; he was a U.S. senator from Missouri and served as Roosevelt's vice president; he ordered the use of atomic bombs against Japan to end the war in 1945; he ended segregation in the armed forces in 1948

WANT TO KNOW MORE?

More Books to Read

Alter, Judy. *Audie Murphy: War Hero and Movie Star*. Abilene, Texas: State
House Press, 2007.

Mazer, Harry. *Heroes Don't Run*. New York: Simon & Schuster Books for
Young Readers, 2005.

Nicholson, Dorinda Makanaonalani. *Remember World War II: Kids Who
Survived Tell Their Stories*. Washington, D.C.: National Geographic
Children's Books, 2005.

Williams, Brian. *Life as a Combat Soldier*. Chicago: Heinemann Library, 2006.

On the Web

For more information on this topic, use FactHound.

1. Go to *www.facthound.com*

2. Type in this book ID: 0756538424

3. Click on the *Fetch It* button.

FactHound will find the best Web sites for you.

On the Road

National World War II Memorial

National Mall

Washington, DC

202/619-7222

Freedom Wall with 4,000 gold stars

to honor 400,000 lives lost

The National World War II Museum

945 Magazine St.

New Orleans, LA 70130

504/527-6012

Personal stories, historic artifacts, and interactive displays

Look for more We the People books about this era:

The 19th Amendment

The Berlin Airlift

The Civil Rights Act of 1964

The Draft Lottery

The Dust Bowl

Ellis Island

The Fall of Saigon

The Great Depression

The Holocaust Museum

The Kent State Shootings

The Korean War

The My Lai Massacre

Navajo Code Talkers

The Negro Leagues

Pearl Harbor

The Persian Gulf War

The San Francisco Earthquake of 1906

Selma's Bloody Sunday

September 11

The Sinking of the USS Indianapolis

The Statue of Liberty

The Tet Offensive

The Titanic

The Tuskegee Airmen

Vietnam Veterans Memorial

Vietnam War POWs

A complete list of We the People titles is available on our Web site:
www.compasspointbooks.com

INDEX

About the Author

Sharon Cromwell lives with her husband and their son in Chester, Connecticut. She has written a number of nonfiction books and many newspaper articles for young readers. She also writes for a weekly newspaper. She loves to read, travel, and spend time with friends.